When the *Trees* STAND STILL

AMELIA WORTHWHILE

WHEN THE TREES STAND STILL

iUniverse books may be ordered through booksellers or by contacting:

iUniverse
1663 Liberty Drive
Bloomington, IN 47403
www.iuniverse.com
844-349-9409

ISBN: 978-1-6632-1252-8 (sc)
ISBN: 978-1-6632-1253-5 (e)

Library of Congress Control Number: 2020921559

Print information available on the last page.

iUniverse rev. date: 10/28/2020

Apotheke.gr
Apotithenai

Gardening grass

be sure,
you can
were poets' poisoners?
Never
poets were not poisoners
but
rest easy.
Where their success depends?
their success depended on
discretion.
they were the quiet ones,
the romantic ones
the least suspicious
going about their business,
going about their everyday life
hanging laundry, putting up fruit preserves,
making tomato paste.
a loaf of bread cooling on the counter.
their gardens were well kept. bright flowers,
butterflies, fresh produce,
grass.

self-sufficient, creative,
they seemed popular.
In moments
visitors came and went.
they really had better things to do
than write poetry.
I never ask them
What, and
I will never know.

things I always thought
were poison, do you?

Is three-leafed plants in July?
Is barberry red, leaves of rhubarb?
Is crabapples?
only dado dakies are poison.
Is wild mushrooms?
Is the powder of monarch butterflies, the
toads, the turtle shells?

blunt-nosed snakes.

Is grasshopper spit?

Is tomato greens, potato eyes?
Is drinking milk outdoors?

Is September? That I always thought were poison?
sharing bubblegum,
touching the underside
of school desks,
inhaling the air over
drinking fountains,
sitting on public toilet seats

Is in every day, life I thought were poison?
drunkards,
jerks, and gigolos
in a thought the whole city was under poison.
the whole city was poison!

is it not? Or why it is?

– a fruit-

In my hand
it is
cold, round, smooth
weighs 4 oz.
like a newborn kitten.
my finger finds a low spot, a cleft
cool to the light touch.

eyes register purple, spherical, give it the name
plum.

bluish tinge around that cleft, a butthole!
funny if your mind goes there.
it fits in my palm, so shiny it reflects
the kitchen lights.

with my thumbnail i puncture the skin,
peel back this labial surface,
scratch out a crease, a furrow
juicy, shallow wanting
sunset rainbow lips of auberge,
crimson, soft gold into the shadows
where a tongue might explore.

teeth suck from
the chin dribble point of view,
the nose of unoaked wine.

the must of damp kisses,
leave no marks on the flesh
behind dark epidermis.

Peeling the barcode
as the barcode label,
an equal patch of skin goes with it
more naked than nude, her
true value exposed.

Large fruit
is it a large piece of fruit?
how do I know a seed is in it?
a pit, deep
i bite away voraciously
looking for that heart.
this is a sticky subject for vivisection.

my fingers tear into the meat
until unpretentious stone.
I have forgotten; about the cyanide.
What fruit was it?

- morning prescription-
reading my coffee mug

my morning meds
line up like little planets
on the counter

iron mars the red pill
tiny low-dose aspirin, mercury
green earth anxiety
blue Neptune pain
venues', white…for?
I don't recall.
The others have names, I can't pronounce
But I think
I do miss Pluto.

- sweets unknown -sweets from England

mistakes happen.
the pharmacist was busy and
sent his assistant to fill the order.
attic, the cask in the corner.
pick one.

oops.
turns out that white stuff
was not powdered gypsum
after all.

had the candy maker just used sugar
like the recipe called for,
this wouldn't have happened.
cheaper filler=quicker killer.
twenty-one dead by morning.
humbug.

new rules: better labeling.
stricter paperwork re: dispensing
of arsenic.

- dirty snow-

sounds like a summer drink
expect vodka, not the runoff of
arctic glaciers
melting under the weight of
chlamydomonas nivalis algae

their microscopic bodies collecting
in sun cups, bloody little puddles
that accelerate the global warmth

but this is not news.
Aristotle wrote of it;
John Ross 200 years ago
sent Baffin samples back to England,
thought he'd caught some meteor fallout.

yet the botany was clear;
the breath and beat of earth is persistent
even as she constantly tries on
new colours and textures.

so dance! refresh from mountain streams
that will long after us
continue to change the shape of oceans.

– easy recipe-

Anonymous name admitted to killing her husband
by spiking his water with toxic levels of tetrahydrozoline,
a key ingredient in eye drops and nasal spray.

You can learn so much on the internet.
Who knew eye drops would get the job done?
You don't need a degree in chemistry;
you don't even have to be able to
pronounce those polysyllabic words on the back of the bottle.
Everything is right there; look it up:
How to poison your spouse slowly. Or quickly.
What does he weigh?

There are mail order instructions
for fabricating a 3-D machine gun
at home.
How to mix common fertilizer products and
blow up office buildings or daycare centers.
Floor plans, exit routes.
Creative inspiration.

- laws of nature-

immortal children
challenge
laws of nature drawn to
scares and dares
like caped

there is no kryptonite
in cinnamon or cigarettes
any shit they'll inhale
just to be approved and
proven

just to show themselves
there's nothing more to fear
street level
what the hell they
pass around a tube of liquid cool
as if still unevolved
their gills can handle it

-cinnamon and its properties

cinnamon floats.
will not absorb liquid.
will not mix into my kefir.
why?
oh.
cinnamon is ground up bark.
it was a tree.
this is how our ancestors made
dugouts.
and canoes.
i am trying to drink a boat.
it is supposed to be good for me.
mostly it sticks to the sides
of the glass.
what we learned in grade 3 social studies:
from 1271 to 1295 Marco polo traveled across asia
in search of silk and spices and he met kublai khan.
when he got home to Venice, he wrote a book
about his adventures.
so i thought Marco polo invented cinnamon.
apparently not.
a prize fit for kings and gods.
Apollo had a deep appreciation.
temple virgins left bowls full.

now picture them on mt. Olympus:
hey, Poseidon – i dare you to

swallow a teaspoon of this stuff in under a minute!
Hermes, are you in?
Athena, the sensible one,
warns of the toxic effects of coumarin and the risk
of asphyxiation or a collapsed lung.
the girl was no fun at parties.
it is told the phoenix builds its nest
from cassia, but
consider this:
a firebird rises from ashes, fully fledged,
no need for eggs. nest.
Mayan chocolate? no such thing.
the Mayans had no knowledge of cinnamon.
another myth
perpetuated by the cruel folks at häagen-dazs.
(Bronx, New York.)
limited edition, they called it, once establishing the
addiction.
so i got an ice cream machine
and learned to make my own.
chai -tea
Cinnabon
pumpkin pie
with cardamom
applesauce
wassail, punch
raisin cookies
after lunch.

– it is a lovely day in the town
-clouds

suspicious green-tinted
silence
rolling
then directed, definite
prepared to kill.

- grilling

scraping the black gunk off the grille
recognize this is what becomes the
steak stripes
lung spots

delicious salt blood dripping
down your chin, your throat,
sometimes with an ice-cold beer
it's easy to enjoy life

- passing the dirt

this shit is in my lungs
that rot and mold i couldn't see
until i began to tear off the linoleum, the
peel and stick tiles, the chipboard,
right down to the beams, the muddy
crawlspace,
darkness.
and at night we depend on our trees
to breathe stardust, filter that pretty zhug island sunset
so on bright blue days we take our own breath for granted
forget what is hidden behind the fluffy white clouds.
-

the death of a friend

in another room, my dog is fighting for her life.
here, the new kitten bounces around as if
i'm her only playmate so whatever i'm doing, she
should be in the middle of it. and i smile.
yesterday i sat on the beach, read for awhile
and conversed with a swan. now i'm coughing and queasy
as i assess the best way to remove the rotting
floor where the washing machine has leaked for
30 years. last night i drank wine and played balderdash
with friends in their bright, cheerful apartment. this morning
i had to carry a 50 lb coonhound down the steps so
she could poop and pee outside--with dignity. i sat on the porch
and i cried.

- water disaster In a town

reasons for the downfall
of the roman empire are still in dispute.
was it really irrigation systems made of lead
that caused madness, infertility, depleted armies?
neither the politicians
nor historians could
reconcile.

i remember when a fire truck would pull up
on hot summer days
and they'd open the hydrants.
all us kids splashed and laughed in the torrent
like there was no tomorrow.

today a utility worker came by
to flush out the hydrant across the street
and a thick canvas hose gushed out to the road,
clear water roiling ankle deep along the curb.

my grandson's face
as he stomped and wallowed in this small deluge
was priceless,
and i said go ahead, enjoy!
it's clean.

–swimming pool pleasure

today they say there's a phosphorescent shine on
the surface of lakes st clair and erie
a result of global warming

like primordial ooze
or was that the original cooling
from whence we came

now we can't go
back

- making wine and bottled it

the potions wizard
slides down to me,
a white rag tossed over his shoulder
like a magic cape.

he says *name your poison*
as i peruse labels,
all the pretty bottles
on the top shelf.

just something to wipe the slate clean.

-Lepidoptera insect

aren't monarch's toxic?
they always ask.
are you a starling, a toad?
or is this strictly human interest?

heed the warning, avia!
leave alone that brilliant
dance macabre sharing sky,
the wings plucked appetizer
to fat abdomen full of cardiac glycosides
a milkweed milk unkind

and you, amphibia, keep your tongue
furled tightly between uncapped jaws,
give careful thought to every tempting teasing
butterfly, run instincts quickly through your
tiny brains before you choose unwisely.

- unknown past

i never knew my grandfather
my father never knew his father
my daughter never knew her father
- a bad choice
not like mustard gas in southern France
not like widowhood in '28 and
families emigrating east
west south to never

my daughter never knew her father
because her father never knew her mother
or should not have
at all but for the results of union,
the mustard gas hot air of his doing
poison words, cancerous legacy
all she seems to get from him,
the money is gone,
the promises are yellow clouds

- glykologia

these bees have feasted on
oleander, every drop will elicit tears
every flower wasted garden

beauty is not priceless, it is a toxin
a flashy warning recognized by certain fauna,
instinct steering them from the notorious

but the bees have been seduced, the wagging
language of one leading to sweet contamination,
the casual ingestion by both passers-by and collectors
of fine poetry, multiple coronaries;
we all succumb to the rhetoric.

- SOS

we are drawn to what is
bad
for us
this one has a skull & crossbones on
~~the bottle~~ his t-shirt
i know better
someone stop me
the colour of ~~the~~ temptation/his eyes
irresistible

i am only a woman
attracted to the open package
of seduction, all the
right promotion on the label,

however.
i am going in.
someone…

call poison control.
the number on the fridge
carved into my headboard.

my eyes looking in mirror- mirrored eyes.

you'd think by now
i'd recognize
vial green
psychopathic eyes
this is not my first moonlight dance

don't moths with their compound perception
notice the fried remnants of other moths
don't their antenna pick up on the sizzle and burn
in time for them to hit reverse
flitter off into the safe dark

i have been drawn before by
killer looks
the charm and serial promise of classic
case studies
you'd think it's easy to turn and run

you'd think

St. George and the dragon

sleeping monster
smothered
years and then
offered casually
once,
an evening's bliss

now i seek him out, see if this is true
see if
i am back
with wings, claws, fangs,
voracious as ever,
he is my addiction

st. George of England
kill me now
before i inflict more pain on myself

i should roar, breathe fire,
retreat to my dry old cave
withdraw
withdraw
withdraw
turn off the lights

refuse
eye contact

someone once called him
heroin
i'm stronger than that

-What is poison-

this may be poison
it looks like poison
tastes like
i imagine
pomegranate
alcohol
on the rocks
so pretty in the glass
a brown red
blood liquified
there should be candles
in case i die

if i die
i want to be looking at you
stand there
right there
smile at me
say *drink slowly*
small sips

listen to this
the tinkle of the ice cubes
so pretty in the glass
a cold burn on the tongue,
iodine down my throat
i love your voice

say it again
drink slowly

hold the glass to my cheek
an icy kiss,
so pretty, the glass
i wonder what's in it

might be poison
let me see your eyes
if i am dying.

- Bella Madonna in early morning.

woman descending staircase
not nude
recognizes overpowering scent
of brugmansia
tries not to open her eyes
ruin sexy dream
trips over cat
cat yowls
eyes open
woman sees herself
in full length mirror
in flannel pajamas
cat wants out
everyone has to pee.

- medieval apotheke

i) Romeo and the apothecarist

There is thy gold, worse poison to men's souls
Doing more murders in this loathsome world
Than these poor compounds that thou may'st not sell.
I sell thee poison, thou hast sold me none.
          (Romeo and Juliet, V.i)

Shakespeare nails it as usual.
To paraphrase an often-disregarded scene:
He finds a dealer closed for the holidays
(these guys sleep late anyway),
bangs on the door to rouse the fellow
comes to the point –

You look hungry, I want something
quick and painless, no one needs to know,
here's forty ducats.

The guy feigns innocence,
puts up a feeble moral argument,
concedes
this gets the job done
quickly.

So Will, what else?
It's not about the drugs
but human greed, a quicker buck
and loophole laws that circumvent what's safe or
environmentally sound, efficiency of value,
profit margins precedent
over biohazards, childlike trust.

Herbicides and rapid-fire semi-automatics
available at Walmart or just down the block,
the house with all the weeds out front
a vital economy to someone.

act

the setting,
here, but similar
to denmark.
i will play ophelia.
as this scene opens
you enter
tragic
triumphant in
your own oblivion.

sinking loveless
but for yourself
i would be those eyes,
lacrimal ponds.

witness your soliloquy
from a dark corner
then wrest from you
a poisoned dagger.

later, in another room
of the castle
we shall toast our kings and mothers!
such convenient allies in deception,
fatal determinants.
the goblet is tossed aside,
an insignificant prop.

yet, what was that potion
tasteless sorcery turned
brine as we wallowed
in the spillage
of what might have been a good year?

who held it to your lips, my love,
who touched your lips?
speechless, knowing
even as the final thrust
drew that warm farewell,
the scene was yours.

Hamlet The King

A short rest, I'll take, here,
one of my favorite after lunch spots.
Under a tree laden with memories of
my son when he was a happy boy.

In this drowse a warmth, a tingle in
my upward ear, the sound of water, waves…
the Baltic blocking out the noise of politics,
my oft stubborn Gertrude.

Dear Gertrude…my heart
slows

I am afraid
you are becoming
the last thing I see
at my eyelids.

---- spiritlessly----A source of youthfully joy

she was a surprise as
a little girl; she liked to play
with snakes,
explore fields and ditches with
her brothers,
play war games,
ignite anthills

and she grew to lead armies, wear
fine lingerie, fearlessly apply
asps to her breast
die every time

this time i will prepare her

romance, medieval time

she kissed him
with tainted lips
as his
tingled, became numb,
the rest of his body responded,
briefly, as would a man
in lust

she allowed his hands
to brush freely
past diamonds
and velvet décolletage,
but
when they gripped deathly at her skirts,
she stepped back, let him drop
to his knees, bow
at her feet

he looked up
for one more loving gaze
her green eyes now
soft danger,

she did bend
and with one slender fingertip
traced his spittle
downwards to his heart.

-wasn't her name queen what?

A cliché, really: lavish banquet table,
everyone dressed to the nines,
the arrogant host getting a little toasted,
sideways glances of his disenchanted wife,
a closeup
of the pretty new amulet hanging at her cleavage.

And then the choker: wine dribbles from his
smirking mouth,
his eyes widen, he clutches his throat, drops the goblet
keels over either behind the head table or
has the last twitch ability to writhe as far as
the dance floor (director's choice)

but there the anguished grimacing, foaming mouth
and snotty tears, there in full view
the shameful puddle
(quick cut to astonished queen)

the final feeble kick of right leg and
glazing over of his eyes...
Yes, a cliché, but won't we all admit
we cheered when Joffrey died?

- memories from long time ago

Trekking through Everglades. It's hot here.

Looking for Fountain of Youth or lush & verdant winter getaway.

Heavily populated by Calusa. Natives unfriendly. Shot in thigh with poisoned arrow.

Probably dying now. I'm only 46. I did not see that coming.

Say hi to kids for me.

> Love, Juan

- the sweet suicide-

post diagnosis, perhaps a tad dramatic:
but there's this mood which
accompanies a death sentence,
a carelessness, *what's it gonna do, kill me?*
attitude. a more leaden foot, less inclination
to pay the phone bill, impulsive
purchases (i really must have that
buzzard gargoyle to mount in my withered maple)

i love mangos. i'm highly allergic ("lethally" might be
an overstatement) but my face would get all red and itchy
and my ear canals and throat would swell up and i could
choke or scratch myself bloody, and perhaps check out...

yet it's like the prisoner deciding on his last meal: for me,
i'm thinkin' escargot for an appetizer, followed by
lobster tails in drawn butter, a nice pasta, garlic bread,
caesar salad (all accompanied by a fine chardonnay)
...gotta be cheesecake or blitz torte for dessert, or both
(hey, i'm dyin' here anyway—damn the cholesterol)

and a mango. i'd like to finish it off with a plump,
bright and sunny fresh-off-the-boat mango. face buried
in pulp, with spicy juice oozing down my chin, my neck,
my cleavage sticky, bees a-circlin',
the glow of that golden meat the final image
to penetrate my ecstatic eyelids,
the light which i will follow.

- domestic pets eat chocolate or sugar?

little bastard ate the box of
valentine Godiva's i'd left out on the coffee table
not the cheaper drug store brand, the good stuff,

I know it was not a horse.

the kind where every one is wrapped in special paper,
each a precious jewel
the treasure map diagram itself a piece
of art, exploration, sheer poetry in the descriptions...
a sweet confirmation of someone's love for me,
a sensual caress of teeth and palate,
an orgasmic blast of flavor...

never mind...
the dog could die at any minute
must run and google chocolate toxicity in dachshunds,
estimate how many he ate based on
how many i had already savored
then figure out how much the dog weighs
vs. how many grams of chocolate are in the box, divide by number
he possibly consumed,
sniff the inside lid for one last aromatic appreciation of this gift.

I knew it was not a horse.

the math is killing me here,
the dog is currently vomiting on the living room rug
and i'm not sure if that's a good thing or not –
encourage vomiting,
do not encourage vomiting, don't panic
nevertheless, there is vomit that must be cleaned up now
and a dog to get to the vet
at least the little bastard doesn't have opposable thumbs
or he surely would have opened that bottle of malbec i was saving
for a romantic friday night, the dog, not the vet

It was relief to find it was not the horse of the neighbors farm.

little bastard
he's 24 lbs x 145 grams consumed, at best
dark or light chocolate?
how the hell do i know which ones he ate
and which ones he vomited,
right, go look at the vomit, determine its colour

white wine should get the stain out,
but i only have that one bottle;
I sure could use a drink then remember it's for friday night.
little bastard, bad dog!

But hurts when you find the box empty.
Specially eaten from your dog.

-does medicine has a funny side?

arsenic will make you sick
ptomaine will annoy you
warfarin might do the trick
nightshade could destroy you.

hemlock's how great thinkers died
a cup of iodine
just pop a cap of cyanide
a dram of solanine.

if that don't kill you so they say
it's sure to make you strong
but don't try this at home, okay?
OKAY?!

Convulsions-
Agitation

- A PAIR shape reminds?

F
R
U
I
T
stakes
are not
poison
are they?
in this brief
scene a half
a dozen pale
yellow chalky
bullets were given
me by some unlikely
high school friends they
can't be lethal wonder why
that fellow died so hard and
foaming when i drove a fertilizer
bomb deep inside his raping mouth
how could i know this had a kick like
arsenic or cyanide the ditch he fell in
sudsing up the fish the frogs & wildlife
compromised I hope they don't find
fingerprints or trace this back
to me in any way it's just a dream.

- over-enjoyment

one summer day
we were sipping blue slushies
sticking out our tongues
laughing, pointing,
wincing with brainfreeze.

that evening i had a rash
around my mouth, my tongue
swelled up, my entire face, neck,
ears, throat
i went to the clinic, lisped,
i think i'm allerdthic to sluthies
and the doctor said, indeed you are.

one winter day the feral kittens went
under the fence, were playing in
the neighbour's driveway,
drank from a blue-green puddle
of leaked antifreeze
and they all died.

And God said
Love thy neighbor.

- Sunday praise

wasn't that a sunday
morning strewn with
kitten
corpses all across the
fresh cut lawns

welcome mats are often lies
and bowls of milk left out for ferals
not to be believed

so close to home another
high school beating shooting
toxic bias

who still teaches children to despise
draw knives
conclusions
it can't happen here
it cannot where
front yards are bright with
potted plants and songbirds

-a declaration

I did it. I'm the one they're looking for.
They won't find me, I blend in. Neighbours
would say I'm just an average guy, quiet…
I keep to myself. Don't ever complain,
don't draw attention.
But I get things done.

So far there've been fourteen cases reported of
dogs dying 'mysteriously' in this part of town.
Most at the dog park. That's easy, just toss bits of chicken
laced with warfarin over the fence as I'm jogging by.
Some stupid mutt's gonna find it.
I don't care what breed, they all gotta go.

Can't stand the racket every night, someone behind me
let's 'is hound dog howl for a half hour
right when I'm tryin' to get to sleep,
I got work in the morning, bud, shut the fuck up!

Once I had a dog.
I was ten, his name was Tigger, but dad bailed on mom,
we couldn't afford the dog. Oh well,
never mind it was like losing a brother. Mom said
he went to a farm. I dunno.
Never got another one.

People spend too much money on them anyway,
there's better things, more important things,
people with problems,
that's where they should be spendin' their money.
Not fuckin' dog parks.

Anyway, first time I tried it, couple years back,
I used ground beef. Raw.
Easy to roll up a meatball with my special spices
and stick it through a hole in the fence.
Bastard used to make such a racket
whenever I went out to my car. Not anymore.
They won't ever catch me. I'm real careful.

—toxic substances

looked up a chart of toxic substances,
there, 'substance', that which
we can physically experience, ingest.
but there are abstractions,
the poisoning of minds.
i'm not clear on technical terms
but i know what i read.
this terror spreading like a virus
is a bottle spilled, leeching into the soil,

the satellite feeds
the air we breathe and the air we absorb
through our natural antennae,
our own electric energy
filters, disseminates…
i realize i fail at explanation,
rely too heavily on
cosmic communication,
vulcan mind melding
used for good, not evil.

political corruption,
global warming, Syrian refugees,
the opioid crisis. big news. an issue, surely,
but a distraction? don't shoot the messenger;
she has her own private beliefs.
but www? well that's a problem.

imagine the globe, such pretty green and blue
now picture it
with every email, Instagram, retweet,
upward pointing thumb,
every post a game of telephone
a fibred optic line from here to there.

is back to the future
unplugged? will that slow the plague
of 280-character babel,
misinformation,
unbelievable photos,
convenient truths?

it is a web. it is a choking mesh
a giant's fishnet trawl we flounder in,
gasping at what
small holes to sky are open
hands stretching
when fins aren't glued to keypads,
glassy eyes imploring the stars
for a way out of this addiction.

schools of fish, the metaphor,
-- a murmuring of blackbirds
rising simultaneously to the heavens
like a choir of hallelujah!

from here it's hard to tell who set them off,
who directs their path?

they follow the guy in front, i guess.
seems like he knows what he's talking about.

- doubting the belief

Africa 1977
"Religion is the sigh of the oppressed creature, the heart of a heartless world, and the soul of soulless conditions. It is the opium of the people." NO NAME

it was not green Kool-Aid, or red, or orange or purple, first
It was a lethal dose of sedatives and potassium cyanide
mixed in a vat with Flavor Aid, a vile brown solution
parents were compelled to swallow
after squirting it by syringe into the mouths of their babies.

It was a last resort for those who'd lost everything,
had nowhere else to go, and were convinced
this would assure their quiet final moment in purgatory,
their arrival in the land they'd been promised, that spiritual haven
where all men and women and children are equal and cooperative,
peaceful and loving.
This would be their revolution, their glorious protest
against politics and prejudice, capitalism and western degradations;
they would be the heroes of utopia.

There is always crying and screaming at revelation;
but there are sometimes those few unconvinced
whose animal instincts make them run off into the jungle
and witness from a safe distance

while good and evil raise their voices in urgent amens,
righteous direction.

This time nine hundred and nine, but another day, a different place,
one more charismatic visionary,
one more wide-eyed pious lineup to sip from a goblet of blood.

– clouds of lilac

.for all the Anonymous Constables

home at noon for lunch,

heard the dark crowd before, it
gathered angrily,
100 teens in dark clothing a turmult
on the muddy spring sod
surging towards the center
and receding to the
chant
two cops ineffective
try to beat off children
like a heartbeat
chant

next sudden flares of purple smoke
someone had explosives, scattered briefly
long enough to see the catalyst
the nucleus a young guy, perhaps 18,
dark haired, long and greasy, empty in his eyes
the blindfold slipping, gag no longer tied
but there he was bound to a kitchen chair with
belts of dynamite across his chest and poof
another crack of lilac smoke another scatter
of the ants and re-assault, thinking they're killing him
or trying to save him, thinking didn't want to know

sirens coming, cops already there
no need to stay to see this then the
chanting
louder as an amp was turned up, words like
'Aquilegia' and 'suffer' and a litany of names
Maybe 7, or 8, or 9
…words fading as running
but not until the boy announce
my name is 10… and
you will all remember me,
you will read this on the front page
…
tomorrow and in
less than a few seconds it will all be over
…

Keeping on running west and looked up lost
to realize the overshot was a block from my house.
a block in flight
from the sounds and image, and never forget that face
hearing his fireworks like missiles
like a flamingo to see what smoke surrounds the buildings,
expecting clouds of lavender

shopping in the mall gardens in July

post apocalypse abandonment
unpotted figs crisscross clutter one aisle
dry dirt, dead leaves
tumble like weeds over
late afternoon concrete open air facing south
for godly or natural intervention –

a drop, just a drop.
you almost hear the cry of crowded marigolds,
see the desperate reach of cucumber vines and
leggy bottom tier tomatoes, stunted eggplants
destined for mulch next week
if management even remembers
to assign staff to clear out seasonal,
take down the steel-grated temporary shelving.

faded golden floribunda
missed the best of its season.
in a proper garden it would have been cultivated,
pruned to ensure rejuvenation,
but here brown leaves curl, petals fall,
i find myself humming yellow rose of texas.

there was one healthy calla lily
hiding in the shade of concord
grapes and blueberry bushes, its single bloom
an exotic, rare black, perfectly undead,

somehow still thriving in this wilted jungle hades and
i wanted to be its salvation, bring it home, find it a place
next to the pond, nurture it as i would all
those once bright beings,

but the gates were closed, padlocked
and no one was around to take my money.

swallowing crumbs

she threw them out for the squirrels
but the squirrels are picky or
sated.
now sparrows and more aggressive starlings,
a grackle

argue
after rain,
over rye and wonder bread heels, stale with
refrigerator burn, torn in
irregular clumps (the jays
have already made off with the larger pieces)

there's a skitter of action
little explosions of feathers
a tussle that draws cats
to the screen door

the alert birds fright,
assess risk, while the weak and desperate
are oblivious
to all but the last defense against starvation

and we know, or it is said
that bread crumbs are bad for birds,
swell in the crop or gullet,
suffocate them.
this could be a lethal charity

--- sailing swans

swallow deep, the blue
oh wild angels
embracing liberty
by nature's grace
you fly

then cut by hunters' lead
you fall through heaven
to your own cold lake.

or sailing like wild lilies, shallow
dancing
dip and scoop the shoreline

swallow deep the dormant lead
and poison bleeds you slowly
into your own cold lake.

– pollution on earth.

pollution, i think
running
out of room
we must change
and grow earth
pull sterile sheets
tighter
perfect hospital corners
and visit often.

ink
blending
bleeding rainbow rivers
flow like rhetoric
write and write and write
before the wells are dry
and presses down
(niagara no longer
falls in mortal servitude.)

the F word.- Or the S word Sheedy sheet
sheet-or swearing in a bad situation

Venomous little bastards!
It's MY back yard.
MY right to move logs, pull the tomato plants,
bring in the lawn ornaments.
You had no territorial signature piss, no brand or
gang tag on the fence warning me…I am an innocent
trespasser; no wait! Who the hell pays the mortgage here?
Yet I'm suddenly attacked by a marauding swarm of stealth stingers,
penetrating my hair, slipping inside sleeves, up and down my t-shirt
as I wail and thrash fuck or sheet- get off me you little fucking or
sheety- bastards
while running for cover and sloughing off my clothes as I make my way to
the porch
and safe, sanctity of my heretofore impermeable wasp-screened house.

My kitten, panic-stricken follows me, trips me
until we find refuge. Breathe.
Get out the baking soda.
Assess the damage in front of the bathroom mirror, (damn, I'm fat!)
Slather on the pasty cure of the 1960's then
watch the black dots rise from my flesh and scrape them off, one by one.

Have a glass of wine, realize I'm still shirtless.
Go upstairs and opt for brown, I'll fool those despicable predators,
I don't care if they have an APB out,
a wanted poster on the inside walls of that tree trunk,
I shall fool them! I am no longer wearing bright pink and
my hands don't smell like lavender soap. I WILL
come back for you, antagonists,
and once you're all safely encamped at sunset,
you will suffer my vengeful wrath by a can of
RAID MAX FLYING INSECT!!
You WILL be vanquished!

– Socrates is dead

my cat socrates ate hemlock
leaves not catnip
three and he
was gone before i got to him

socrates: a common name for cats
not too bright this one
don't ever name your cat
after a dead philosopher

his whiskered face contorted
covered by a diplomatic
cloth of black
some questions plague me.

. --- was Socrates a cat?

Night before last, I was in my office ready to shut down my genealogy research at midnight. Exhausted. CRASH thunder, dog comes running. Tattles.

Out in the living room at the foot of the stairs I find a gallon of topsoil, 87 feet of tangled philodendron, all the clean laundry that had been waiting to go up the stairs, and two black cats slinking away, mud-bellies dragging through the kitchen. Somebody had thought it might be fun to jump from the bedroom windowsill to the top of the dresser, and if she aimed just right, could land between the spider plant and the aforementioned philodendron.

Forty-five minutes it took me to sweep, sort for re-laundering, wipe walls, clean off and straighten artwork and replant aforementioned philodendron.

This morning, I am awakened at 6 am by the sound of a cat retching, hacking, gagging,... at the foot of my bed. Seriously? Get out! Leave me alone!

Three hours later, it is day and I am pleased by how easily the combination of hairball/expectorate lifts off the carpet. Most likely due to the fibre content of aforementioned hairball/expectorate. Its texture was stringy, its tinge rather greenish, a bit like philodendron. (Those things are hard to kill.)

Petite Angelique-or herb de saint Gérard

decked out in hazmat gear,
shower cap, rubber boots, elbow-length gloves

i'm game
i'm eager
i attack
i shall vanquish my foe!

and i pull every noxious weed from its root,
conscious of the potential brush of the flower
against my cheek, a misstep,
headlong pitch into the garden

anxiety builds
there's a clock on this sortie
30 minutes and out, then 15 minutes cold shower

i clutch at clumps with both hands, pull firmly,
discard in bin that must be sterilized afterwards,
move on to the next section,
feel my heart beat faster, glance up
to appraise the competition still standing
must kill must kill!

panting, i wonder
if the pollen or fumes are at that very moment
infiltrating my lungs,
dooming me like mustard gas

must kill!
i see the three leaves hiding within creeping charlie,
under rose bushes, camouflaged in hostas,
must kill, must kill everything!
level the playing field
bare ground
i want bare ground, no place for the bastard enemy
to conceal its evil intent
my wheezing becomes erratic, panicked,
my back aching from refusal to stand up straight
until it's over

and i can finally head for the porch
stripping off layers as i go
clothes inside out gingerly dumped in a trash can
enter the house with my hands held surgeon-like
touch nothing, leave not a germ
between here and the shower
destroy! destroy!
the loofah leaves me raw,
the cold water restores my breathing

but now i wait for
the inevitable reaction

- symptoms of organ failure

my skin is malfunctioning.
it is no longer protecting my heart, lungs, muscles, bones.
nerves.

fire ants under my
crimson-stippled flesh
leap synapse to synapse.
following the trail of my fingernails
as i engrave my entire body with this misery.

here is a red pen, what if
i use it to scratch and let it
scribble along the zigzag conduit,
note the mirroring: left ankle,
now right ankle, left shin, right shin,
left behind-the knee (does that body part even have a name?)
right behind-the-knee,
left inner thigh, right inner thigh
onwards and upwards, i think you get the picture.

it is impolite to scratch in public.

this red pen is on its way
to poetry.

– the taster of the King

i am not to be admired
for my job, a taster to the king.
you see the nightly feasts,
his arrogant gut,
believe that ev'ry rich, exotic dish i sample
must bring joy to my palate.
your tongue lolls in awe at stories of
the bloodiest venison, creamy pastries,
gifts of sweets and rare liqueurs
from foreign potentates,
each meal a celebration of some
politicking underway.

you wonder why i've not
gained twice my weight this month,
i'll tell you:
actually, i have a nervous stomach.
i'm not hungry, and yet, yes, i am.
just once i'd like a meal prepared by mother,
trusted milk and pablum of my innocence,
but now i cringe,
approach each dish or cup in service
and take a cautious sip, a nibble

risk my very life on his behalf.
the task is in the tasting,
not for me to say if gluttony will be
the true assessment, potency is so variable.
i'm there only to sniff and swallow.
if i seem fine, he'll dine,
but if i die on site
(a job well done),
he fires the kitchen staff
and everybody starves.

Laced - entangled -interweaved- linked named it

sugar daddy
arm candy
trophy wife
trick or
treat suck this
you don't know where it's been
what it has been dipped in.

five second rule
head thrown back ahhh!
aha!
sleep now, my love.

this can't be traced
the tears will be real
the gossip short-lived.

- Fatality among women
Locusta

there is a herstory
of belladonnas and black widows
a few drops to dilate the pupils
make seductive bedroom glances,
flirting
the second oldest opportunity
to advance a girl's career

she learned to cook with deadly
nightshade, seasoned mushrooms, and
if all else fails a feather tainted
down the throat of rich old men
will look like mercy to the courts
if
all accomplices
are trusted.

Water Tofana

here darling, try a spritz
oh, not your scent then
how about my line of fine cosmetics,
brighten your complexion?

this! my signature blend
of special herbs and elements of
nature don't you love
the little makeup jar it
comes in?
set in right there on your
vanity in open view
your man will not suspect
three tiny drops
tipped in his after dinner cordial.

a noble calling, the poisoner
her mortar, pestle,
cauldron,
implements archaic kitchenware
her back door busy with the likes of
Agrippina and a queue of many Mrs. Caesars.

The lady Borgia

with this ring
i am associated
mythologized
accused

only a hollow ring
custom made, a gift from my father
something to kiss

for those several husbands
heads bent, genuflecting before me,
it was my hair, i tell you
my perfect skin and long pale neck,
handful breasts
and the way i taught myself to float across a room,
above the intrigue

like a feather,
a piece of the tapestry,
brush strokes and papal bull
the soirees
orgies
rumours
all art.

i had ten babies, more lost
than blessed.
i assure you
with my belly in a constant state of swelling
this ring
does not fit.

the angel of Nagore

there was a time, a generation
of women who learned
the fastest way to be a
merry widow

was to boil a sheet of flypaper,
scrape off the sticky arsenic,
perhaps use it in pastry

make angels out of monsters.
give themselves
some breathing room.

Diane de Poitiers
French lady

her body exhumed, golden hair
analyzed found laced with
aurum potable
elixir of the gods, mere mortals seeking
vain eternal youth
that certain glow from within
sipped potions made of metals
magic said to be insoluble
juice of fennel, wines and mothers' milk
as diluent
a morning cocktail picker-upper
colour of mimosas sunshine paradise
the promise of alchemy still enticing
vials sold by gram and carat
incantations latinized for authenticity
the side effects downplayed, the fevers, salivation,
sweat and kidney damage contraindications
merely inconvenient sacrifices
one must suffer to achieve an everlasting beauty,
such a lovely corpse.

–sinful Human values

So, who is truly without sin;
isn't that the point of apples?
They hang from trees like ovaries, testicles
tempted by gravity to fall.

The fallen: Eve, Snow White?
Or was it the vengeance of some evil witch,
was it the crime of the jealous, ignorant,
the indifferent,
the know-it-alls
who couldn't break the code and save the world
without him?

A man ends the war
and is castrated for his troubles.
No ticker tape parade, no turn the other way,
gracious acceptance,
no *love is love is love* in postwar England
where Newton's genius was lauded
but Turing's was tainted, criminal,
not considered history book heroic,
not an influence appropriate
for prep school lads,
yet not something just
given its due privacy.

I think Alan saw the poetry of poisoned apples
when he solved his last
equation.

– The Rank of the third Empire
Helga Goebbels

perfect little Nazis
obedient to the father
land
we had our pictures taken with der Fuehrer
our hands not quite level practiced often
posing fair haired

I'm twelve, the oldest of my siblings
and aware of tension,
suspicious of the stories of inoculation
the safe place we're going to, the sweetened drinks
we were all having, sitting around a table in our nightgowns
in the bunker while mother brushed our hair,
put in matching ribbons

I start to cry softly when she says
bedtime, guiding drowsy
up the stairs, her little lambs and
promises them each a candy
once they're all tucked in

I resist and she is pushing me
to help her with the young ones
come be a good girl now
she gives them little capsules tells them
bite down, swallow, sleep my babies

but Helmut's tiny twitching body,
saliva bubbling from Hedda's mouth
scares me and I scream
what are you doing!
try to shake my sisters conscious,
mother slaps me asks me would i rather be
held hostage, raped by Russians, tortured
this my darling is the better way you'll be
reincarnated, have a nicer life
she corners me and tries to
shove it down my throat I'm biting begging
mama please! where's daddy!
daddy where are you?
someone can't you stop her
mommy no!
I clench my teeth
she pries her nails into my cheeks
forces fingers in my mouth
my head is twisted
crack
I feel the agonizing fracture
of my jaw
white pain
my breathing

lady Goering

Hermann was an art aficionado,
amounted his private collection, they say
by looting and corruption,
a man needs to
hang
Renoirs and Van Goghs somewhere,
his country estate catalogue shows someone
of great sophistication and refined tastes.
(this was not his most heinous of crimes)

yet is it plausible a gentleman like this
might conceal a vial of cyanide within his rectum, or
jam it under one loose gold crown, into his navel,
tape it between folds of belly fat,
where is the dignity in that
attempt to cheat the common noose?

more likely is romance, mystery,
the theories around bribery, prison guards succumbing
to seductive strangers, delivering secret messages
and medications in fountain pens,
or
the fairy tale death kiss his wife bestowed
the night before.

yes, I was allowed in for a few moments,
a courtesy, a
tradition, one last whispered farewell
lips pressed between the prison bars our
tongues entangled he found the small memento
I brought him
hidden inside my cheek.

Lady Braun

If I'd made a movie of the last few days
it would not be the romance you all imagined, a
joyful wedding between two people who had
carried out a quiet passion for years;
his image and career were always the priority.

But he cared for me, took care of me, provided
the life of a queen where I was free to pursue my
own interests – shopping, taking pictures,
playing with Negus and Stasi
and a few times a week we'd be together.
I'd help him unwind

He never talked about work, really, and of course I had
some knowledge of his position, his importance, but
politics didn't really interest me.
My Wolf was such a handsome man.

In early April, as you know, the war was pressing closer
so by midmonth he had me brought to the bunker.
The place was crowded and damp,
the smell of mold and sound of water pumps pervasive,
and our only glimpse of sunshine was on
his birthday, when we took what would be
a last stroll with our dogs in the chancellery garden.

After that the tension became unbearable,
the outcome Inevitable.
But I would not leave him. I would be his wife,
at his side until the end.
A short civil ceremony,
he goes off to rewrite his will,
then we have our brief honeymoon.

In the morning we host a wedding breakfast
and he orders cyanide for Blondi. Just to be certain.
Distraught over the dog; we retire to his sitting room
where I offer final consolation.

the leaves fall from the tree all year around!

i feel compelled to disrobe,
this could be eden
an orchard of delicious
falling
at my feet
my gaze
the scent of warm pie and horses
near.

there are pickers a few rows over,
hands stamped, authorized and joyous
but i have not paid.

i tell myself
it would be_____
what is the word,
has it yet been created?

i am not starving, it's just that
they are so available,
ripe, bounteous
who would notice
the absence of one windfall?

i look for venomous snakes,
expect a farmer with a musket.

i sit under a heavy limb
with my purse open,
awaiting providence, resisting.
thinking,
so far
i'm better at this than eve.

-- Paradise

close enough.
all i deserved.
there's a fine apple tree at least.

your own gardens turn.
there are things that will bite
rash, choke your sinuses and your lungs
quietly cut limbs.

i am barely clothed
in this privacy
assert myself,
talk to the air around me
reminded of life lessons, take care
of
you
repeat mantras, i am a good person
i am a worthy person, i do love me.

gardening is busywork. a distraction.
a justification for something one calls solitude when
the ugly reality is loneliness.
the trees talk back in my own imagined voices,
he said she saids.

reclined in sun-shone grass to pull creeping charlie,
move planter pots for better light,
anger the armies of woodlouse, centipedes,
everything runs away.

there are irritants here.
count the days until there might be an allergic reaction
bad enough to isolate you even further, blisters itching
up legs, arms, face.
nobody thinks you're pretty.
is this called mindfulness? i've seen the posters.
a new meme for what poets have done all along.

blood in the dirt. oh.
five minutes ago a branch had snapped
against my ungloved pinky finger and i squeaked
but no bother, carried on, determined to finish along this fence.
when i try to stand up
every loud and arthritic body part participates.
then the earth turns, clouds cloud, arms dance for balance
as i am being cast out
a subtle message that i don't belong.

blood and dirt on my hands. oh.

Antidotes-
Remedies

when the earth has an hour in year

– Year 2009

earth hour minute forty-eight,
by candlelight and crown royal,
i spy on neighbours well-lit all
and righteous, smugly tsk tsk

ill-informed they go about
with naïve entitlement, breed
carbon-guzzling replications
of their faulty gene pool,
dump their garbage this side of the tracks
rather than neatly at the curb
on tuesday night
blue box red box colour blind
no matter, it floats down the river
after dark

we wonder who could who would
why on earth but
i can tell you now, at eight-fifteen
their lights were shining oh so brightly.

—Year 2013 leo

fish by candlelight
are slow and sequined,
clown-spotted, herringbone
patterns – their deliberate skins
countable
remind me of multiplication tables

they gather at their glass wall like
moths intrigued, bewildered
by this new luminescence
their black eyes and
borp, borp, borping mouths quietly
asking if i have an explanation.

.

-year 2015

some people don't care
or know. nor would they care if they knew.
these are the right-to-lighters among us.
those who fail to realize what a luxury it is
to have electricity, or how fortunate we are
to live here and not have to walk two miles
carrying jugs of questionable well water.
it's hard to know who to pity, or to despise.
random genealogy landed us here
and not in some third world country;
in either place only the strong survive.
i guess it's about attitude.

so turn off your lights at least as a show
of grace and humility. take just one hour
out of your busy year to consider your dumb luck.

-From the earth

bobbing
in the kitchen sink
all the ground apples
and the last hangers on,
one final batch
to simmer in cloves, cinnamon,
a pinch of salt.

these were not beautiful,
not a single ontario no.1 grade in the basket,
but i've known them since april blossoms,
bee food,
a pale pink cloud floating in my own backyard.
this tree's name is johnny d.
d for delicious.

i only guide nature's selection
letting the weaker drop unfinished,
set my dog on bird and squirrel duty,
drain the fish pond water into the roots.
that's all.
i've already made two pies;
i've not been stung.

a half bushel to pare, core,
cut around blemishes,
worm holes
gaping bites left by blue jays.
we share the same fruit.

– the wanderer

streetwise castoff
you come this far arm's length
twice shy.

take suspect tidbits and kind words like
maybe somedays
but cower retreat disappear for days
if it starts to get personal.

this is what i am offering you:
banquets and fidelity
companionship, a warm bed
a forever home.

here you won't starve
be kicked
left out in the rain,
here you will have a place,
be part of a family,
find love.

with my bare hand
i extend this chance
to trust again.

helping hands

i'm getting grandma hands
wrinkly, blue-veined, arthritic
toad hands
bumpy brown warty hands.

toad warts give you poison
we always heard.

these hands make cookies
pull up zippers, tie shoes
brush hair
these hands will help you
cross the street safely.

-swimming next to octopus

Year 2015
Ikaria

there could be worse things
than to have your friend pee on your foot
i suppose as long as you didn't lose your bikini top
in the surf it is an act of kind compassion try not to look
down at where it's coming from believe relief is like a warm
spilled margarita sticky tinkle trickling salt-rimed fruity
anesthetic

someone	a temporary horror	while hobbling
snapping	just imagine viral infamy	as down the beach
posting	you that woman screaming	on the plane ride home
instagram	*man o war! man o war!*	the pointing
embarrassment	becomes a weekend meme	& the snickering

is really all in good fun

– the advantages and disadvantages
of the asparagus plant

There's nothing as vile as asparagus pee
at 6.59 or at 4.53.

You forget it was dinner so while on the pot
you believe you are ill but you're really quite not.

On sale this week only, for $1.49,
its tender young spring tips delicious, sublime,

And healthy, packed with fiber, B6, and potassium.
It's worth the disgrace of a sulfurous epigastrium.

The Formula

had i taken chemistry i might understand how
mustard gas in wwl killed my grandfather
five years after he got home safely,
how regimes freely expose their own citizens to sarin,
horrific weapons of biowarfare,
how gassing strangers on a subway will cause
change.

i might grasp those real-world spy stories of
gloved handshakes, victims dropping dead
in hotel lobbies
and how white powder in an envelope can
create so much havoc.

had i taken chemistry in high school
those complicated formulae and comparative dosages
of generic painkillers vs. opioids would make more sense
and i'd have a better grasp of the situation, avoid potential
danger

and had i taken chemistry back then
maybe i'd get how antivaxxers justify their position.
it would be easier to accept the poison prescribed;
that which doesn't kill you makes you stronger
and trust all that is good in science.

Protecting children

little girls dressed up for school back then.
my favorite lavender crinoline made me feel like
a princess, all puffed out and as important as
the job our daddy gave us sometimes after dinner.
here's another plastic bottle, try to open it
and get the candies.
but if we did he felt he'd lost
and would come back a week later with
a different kind of candy, a new plastic bottle.

we had no idea this game was science,
didn't know about the kids
our father pumped full of activated charcoal
every other night
when some frantic parent had to call poison control,
be told to rush the child to the nearest hospital,
how many pills do you think he swallowed, ma'am?

'til the time my sister and i were stumped, so flustered
that we couldn't get this one open,
pressing down until our palms had dented circles,
twisting every way and upside down,
what is this puzzle daddy, why can't we have the candy?
we even tried a pair of pliers,
but he said to smash it with a hammer would be cheating.

good girls, yes,
i think you've done it!
i'll have your mother take you downtown for new dresses.

we were never told our job was saving lives
as daddy's guinea pigs, testing the safety caps he made
to keep bad candies out of small mouths.

Acting your role

would you go through that
revolving door once
a week,
sit quietly reading while
your chest is punctured
then the blue blast of
cold poison
infiltrates
every
last
nerve?

could you convince yourself
it's just a fraction of your life
that will totally suck?

given a choice
would you cry, deny,
bargain with the red devil
dripping venom through your veins
intent on wracking your guts with
promissory vomit?

would you believe in science or
pray
for a more gentle
solution?
would you write love letters
and final bequests
or request a redo, another chance
even if it means trading your eyelashes
for a breast,

putting your plans on
hold
to engage in the *courageous battle*
everyone else
talks about.

would you,
given a choice, could you
do what must be done?

-observing the sky

sun in libra
shines on Chiron the centaur,
there by blood, by poisoned arrow,
crafted by his own hand.

it was all a huge mistake, wasn't it?
opening that Pandora's box,
opening that sacred barrel of wine.
the scent of decadence, amorality,
half humanity storms the doors of
anarchy, drunk on Dionysian freedom.
someone must shut it down, a hero
with a deadly quiver
herculean nerve.

there is always fallout.
the ricochet of well-meaning,
the victims always the innocent.
Chiron, fight! through the dreadful pain of
immortality,
powerless
to heal the real issue, the system itself,
multi-headed hydras and executive mandate
powers that be
stagnant
the law of the land,
and Olympus.

you know, sometimes deals are made.
we have another prisoner
suffering
trade your heritage for his freedom
barter away that immortality and
die in peace, let a good man carry on...

go and balance the constellations.

The girl of Priam

From greek mythology

do we even heed prophets on parapets
or dismiss them as troublemakers,
lunatics,
assume agendas,
judge them
to be the puppets of capitalism?

why are the whistleblowers considered hostile
witnesses; have we become so cynical
we don't believe in altruism,
we don't believe the honest truth?

it's a wonder that humanity survived this long
with its capacity for denial, collective egotism
accepting trojan horses,
walking into gas chambers,
clocking in for the afternoon shift at bhopal
or three-mile island,
dancing on the bridge,
catching nuclear snowflakes on their tongues
while watching Chernobyl burn.

will we even know when?
we are being annihilated,
or have we already been warned?
too late, no doubt,
but can we not recognize that
somebody knows
something?

-the new mouse of the dessert

isis or the syrians are taking over or
have taken new york city and may or
may not next want canada are or are
not heading for toronto and we are or
are not mice or rats, but not cartoon mice or
rats although we (i and another mouse or
rat brother) need to run or
accept what is inevitable but

we have seen the dystopic films, read books,
know that freedom is at the discretion of the captors yet
there is always someone outside looking in or
possible liberators so i find a pencil,
a large lead number 2 pencil
and they laugh at me

o did i mention i am a mouse or rat
gnawing on the tip to make it sharp
no matter, i can do that later when we need it
meantime just like seen in films like fahrenheit 451 or
mockingjay or brave new world i know i should hide
my pencil which is as tall as i am
a standing up mouse and i struggle to hold it in my paws
and rodent teeth while climbing a gym class rope
and dropping down the other side
a church or ship or warehouse full of broken entertainment
units flat screen tvs here's a good place

and someone said a pen is better though i prefer
the long term storage properties of lead, no
thanks the ink may dry out, this will be there when
we need it

find a dry corner under something that won't move or
be inspected looted pillaged plundered or
confiscated just like in the movies
a major plot device the mission back to where
we stowed the tools we need for freedom,
surely you've seen how these stories play out?
but this time i was a mouse or rat.

- First oath in a relation

Dear so....
i love you enough to
hike in mountains
impale worms on your hook
sleep beside you in a tent
brave the night howling's
and nearby rummaging's

i love you enough
to hand you whatever i must hand you
and cover my ears
let you be the man
while i trust

or in the worst-case scenario
bind your mauled and broken leg
with sticks and pantyhose
suck venom from a snakebite
spit it out like a saturday matinee hero
and haul you on my back to civilization

but darling,
still, there are some things
i will not do.

-the cow-boy

I learned this from john Wayne –
Suck and spit

or one of those 60's black & white cowboy flicks
Suck and spit

probably on a Saturday afternoon
and it's something that stays with you;
Suck and spit

the remedy for a snake bite-, catching it on time
Suck and spit
not the bottle with the skull & crossbones hawked by carpetbaggers
preaching multiple medicinal values from hair growth to
a cure for gout, saddle sores or more delicate complaints
from the back of a wagon.

no I mean good old rattlesnake,
the curled-up cliché hidden in a boot or
behind that particular rock the cowboy uses as a pillow
the maracas we all heard
before we saw it coming.

and lucky for our hero his pal was there to perform the favor
on a most unreachable appendage:

get out your rusty razor or switchblade, give it a good wipe
across your filthy dungarees, then quickly nick an X over each fang puncture,

now you have to suck and spit, suck and spit, be sure not to swallow
suck and spit, 'til I don't know,
they never said when to quit;
how much venom-thick blood must one extract
and
to be sure the hero doesn't fade to black?
drama.

if I ever find myself camping perhaps useful information
left of the Mississippi, somewhere outside dodge or Laramie or Abilene.

a place infested by scorpions and buzzards and rattlesnakes.
a horse's skull beside every man-shaped cactus,
a blazing sun setting in the wild - wild west.

Personal Notes Page

Fishing by candlelight

The sea at night needs a small light
The movement is slow and sequined
A clown spotted is it a herringbone patterns
Their deliberate skins are countable
Remind me of multiplication tables
They gather at their glass wall like
Moths intrigued bewildered
By this new luminescence
Their black eyes and
Burp, burp, burping mouths with tranquility
Asking if I have?
An excuse.

2 Vanilla Fields

Spring, is it Irish?
Fields are grown vanilla?
Or is the season's smelling aroma?
                    Caterpillars and its dill
                            Cool as a watermelon
                                        Pink sweet
                            Sandy beach is it sunny?
Mm! slightly fishy
Something disagreeable is happening
Maddie thought was black and white
But might have been bad food
Vinegar helps
Dirt stillness finally rain is coming.

Swallowed by who?

A small pebble swallowed by
A human?
A bird?
A fish?
To the animal's aids digestion
To Human's settle in the stomach
The Doctor's suggest a little white pill
To perform a medicinal function
by making easier to take it down
the situation, you think would rather bite us in the ass
then let be chewed up and break our death:
Irritants so many;
To talk about them
Is hard.
Sinking.
Cud.
Pearls.
They all do it.

4 The helmet headed kid

Today
I found a broken bird nest fallen
From their wooden forest tree
I ask my self blue jays or robins?
Peculiar people
One helmet-headed kid
Another appears after lockdown, in winter
Seem like bears hanking out of the den
Never listen to the mother
Saying
Wait for daddy he will be out to lift you
So he will put you back to your tree.

Epitaph for Ophelia

Oh! Ophelia a Lady of grace.
A sweet voice a soft hand.
A lover, a daughter.
Hopelessly, mad had gone.
Mourning the loss of her father.
Climbing trees, singing songs.
Thinking of Wonderland!
At an innocent fall, a lily in the river became!
Oh God, She drowns into eternity.
Oh, Mother Earth; is the fair Ophelia there?

Epitaph for Hamlet the Prince.

Hamlet the Prince is dead. You know!
Knowledge was to be his deadly friend.
Then, knowledge has no rules in man.
Stranger you know! In front, of the iron gate of fate,
The seeds of time were not sown.
The see breeze murmured to the stone Tree,
The cloud never cries over the Throne deeds.
Hamlet was to be the King.
Now, how to love Hamlet the King?
Like a sincere dead man of the human race.

Note: This epitaph is for King's Hamlet son. Who died revenging his father's death.
Knowledge: looking for evidence for his father's death.
Gate of Fate: We do not know our fate has a gate in front of it.

Epitaph for Zoe

I never thought I would lie beneath.
Before is happening
I write a few words about muself
I was moving and living my life.
I wandered lonely as a flower petal.
Lonely, as the flowers my mother grew.
Their sweet-smelling went over the hills, over the seas.
Now I remember, Jasmin and Gardenia.
Will I meet my parents in the garden of heaven?
I became a wife to a friend!
Together we had two kids.
God certainly had blessed my earthly life after all.
What else do I want?

Note: Thank you.

Lightning Source UK Ltd.
Milton Keynes UK
UKHW010634171120
373555UK00001B/85